LEGAL NOTICE & INTELLECTUAL PROPERTY RIGHTS

The characters Luna, Leo, and Soggy Toast, including their names, stories, catchphrases, and distinctive visual likenesses, are the exclusive Intellectual Property of Jazzy B Enterprises LLC. Unauthorized use, reproduction, or creation of derivative works is strictly prohibited.

DISCLAIMER

This book is a work of fiction and metaphor. The "magic beans" described are for storytelling and educational inspiration only. The author and publisher are not responsible for any actual gardening mishaps or fluctuating fortunes in the stock market. These beans are not a substitute for cookies.

Published by Jazzy B Enterprises LLC
An imprint of The Magic Bean Academy LLC

ISBN: 978-1-972712-03-0

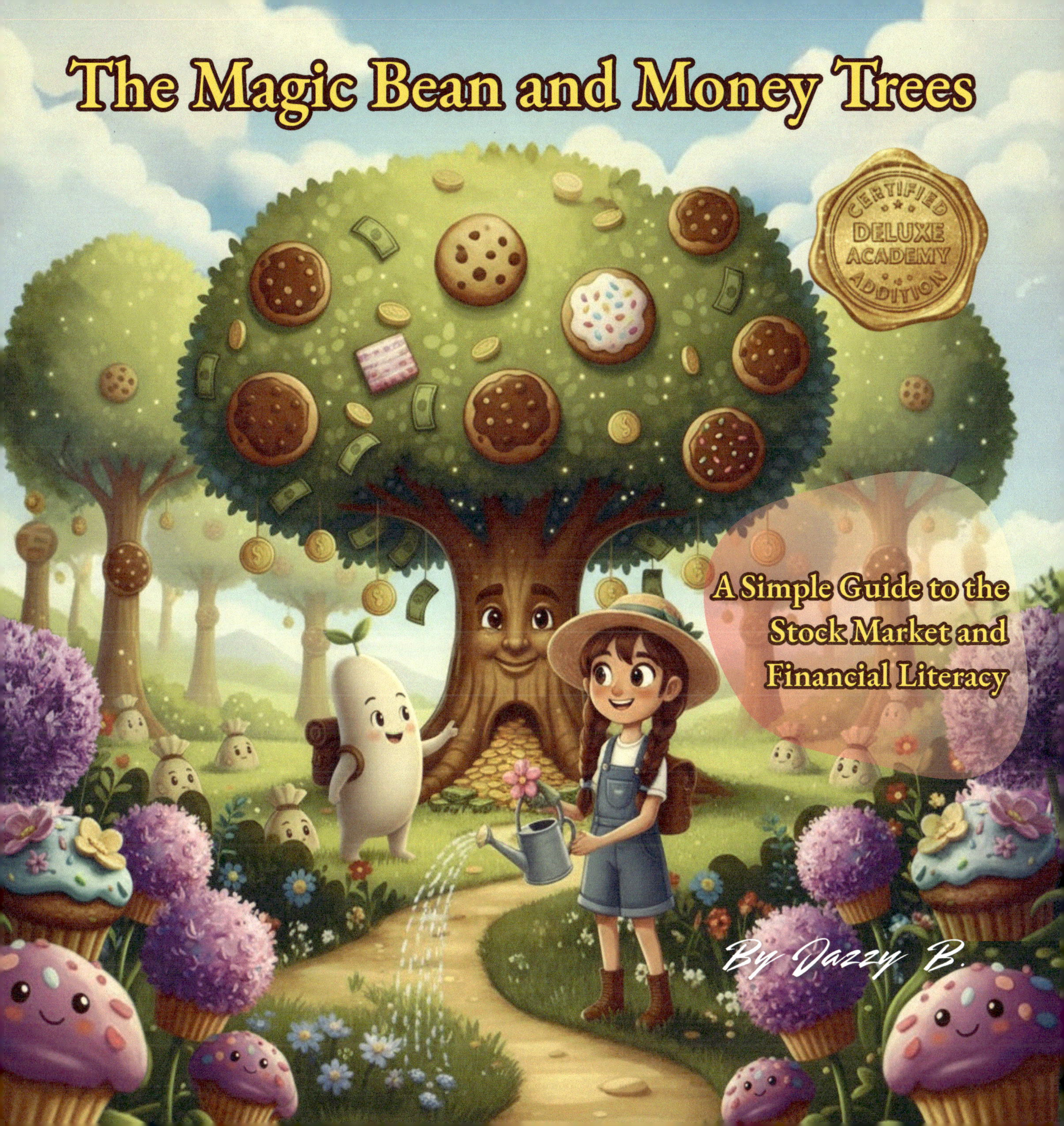
The Magic Bean and Money Trees
CERTIFIED
DELUXE
ACADEMY
ADDITION
A Simple Guide to the
Stock Market and
Financial Literacy
By Jazzy B.

Dedicated to the future Smart Gardeners of the World.

The playground is yours—keep planting, keep learning, and never stop believing in the magic of a single bean. Go grow something magnificent!"

A Letter from the Author

(To the Parents, Teachers, and Big-Hearted Mentors)

Once upon a time, talking about money felt like a chore. It was full of dusty ledgers, confusing charts, and words that felt like a different language. But for a child, the world is already full of magic and growth.

We wrote The Magic Beans & Money Trees because we believe that financial literacy isn't about "getting rich"—it's about planting a garden for the future. By teaching Leo and Luna (and your little reader) that a stock is a "seed" and a portfolio is a "forest," we turn the scary Stock Market into an Investment Playground.

When a child understands that time is "the sun" and a dividend is a "thank-you cookie," they stop being afraid of the unknown. They start to see themselves as Smart Gardeners of their own lives.

So, grab a watering can (and maybe a real cookie), and let's start planting.

"The best time to plant a tree was twenty years ago; the second best time is today."

Happy Growing!

Smart Gardener
Leon Howard AKA
Wallstreet Trapper

To My Mentor, Leon Howard, AKA The Wallstreet Trapper:

"Wealth is no longer a secret; it's a system. And we are the architects."

Thank you for teaching us that we don't just work for the "Cookie Factory"—we own it. You explained the "Big Forest" in terms we can all understand, and your guidance turned my tiny seeds into a thriving garden. Because of your vision, a new generation of Smart Gardeners and their families are learning to turn their seeds into forests and their lives into a lasting legacy.

"Wall Street Looks Like US Now."

To My Patreon Family: Thank you for being the fertile soil that helped my ideas take root. You are the community that proves we don't have to figure it out alone. Together, we've turned our curiosity into a thriving garden of wealth—Together We Thrive, Together We Grow.

Bloom together

Trading Queens: We started as students and became a Financial Freedom Family.

To Our Founder: For leading with beauty, brains, and unmatched elegance.

To the Educator: Thank you for the inspiration to "explain it like I'm five"—that simple wisdom is what started this entire journey.

To my Day One: Thank you for believing in me and supporting my vision from the very first sprout.

To the Quiet Legacy: Thank you for proving that an introverted soul can build the loudest and most lasting legacy in the market.

To the Connector: Thank you for bridging the distance and keeping our sisterhood strong across the digital world.

To the Chart Master: For your mastery of the markets and for always bringing a laugh to the heavy lifting.

It is an honor to be surrounded by such professional, powerhouse women.
We don't just grow alone—**we bloom together!**

Table of Contents

The Beginning of the Journey

"Hello, Explorers!

I'm Jazzy B, your Fairy Queen of Finance and Guide. I've been waiting for you here at the Magic Bean Academy!

In my hand, I hold a tiny, glowing golden bean. It might look small, but with a little magic, it can grow into a massive Money Tree!

I'm not alone on this journey—my favorite students, Luna (the bravest gardener I know) and Leo (the happiest little bean in the forest), are ready to show you the way. Together, we'll teach you the secret codes to grow a garden of your own.
Are you ready? Turn the page and let's find your first bean!"

Chapter 1
The Glow in the Garden Shed
(Owning a Piece)

The sun peeked through the dusty windows of the Garden Shed. This was Luna's favorite place—a cozy wooden shed filled with terracotta pots, silver watering cans, and the sweet smell of damp earth.

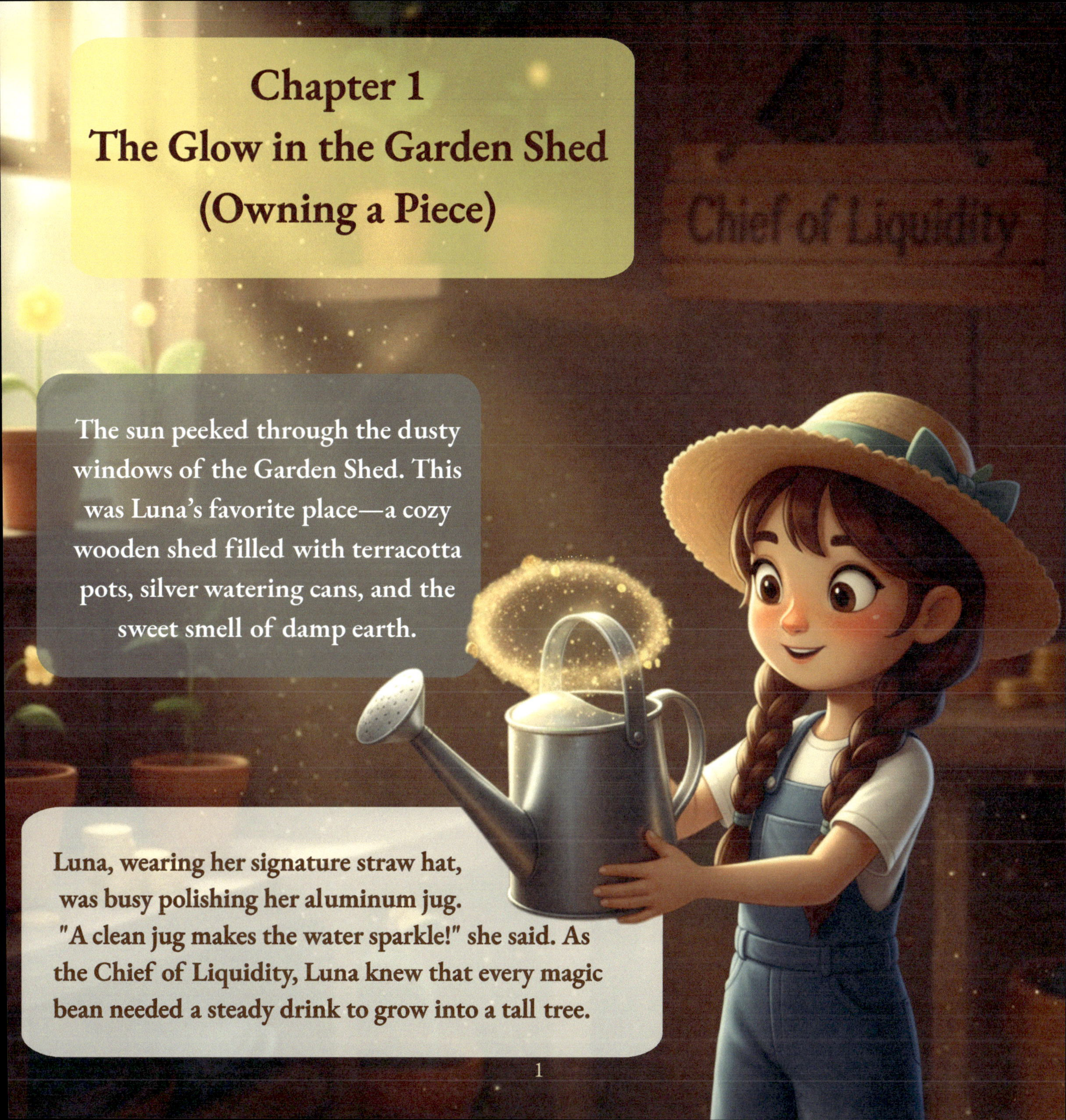

Luna, wearing her signature straw hat, was busy polishing her aluminum jug. "A clean jug makes the water sparkle!" she said. As the Chief of Liquidity, Luna knew that every magic bean needed a steady drink to grow into a tall tree.

Besides her standing in a stack of books, was Leo. He was a little white lima bean with a very big job. He adjusted his leather backpack and watched his Magic Sprout.

Suddenly, the sprout began to wiggle and glow, pointing straight at the potting bench!

"Luna! The Sprout is dancing!" Leo squeaked.

Just then, Jazzy B, the Fairy Queen of Finance, stepped into the shade. She didn't have wings, but her presence made the whole shed shimmer with gold dust. She carried a basket of glowing seeds

"Good morning, Smart Gardeners," Jazzy B whispered. "The garden has a secret to share. Reach into your pockets..."

Leo and Luna reached in and pulled out a tiny, glowing golden bean.

"Most people see a plain seed," Jazzy B said, her eyes twinkling.

"But a Smart Gardener sees a giant tree made of chocolate chip cookies! This bean is a Stock. It's a tiny piece of a real-life magic factory that you get to help grow."

YOUR TURN: Close your eyes and imagine your favorite treat. If you planted a magic bean today, would it grow into a Cupcake Tree, a Lego Bush, or a Sneaker Vine? Draw your dream tree in the air with your finger!
The Secret: A Stock is just like that bean. When you buy one, you become a part-owner of a real factory.

Spaceship Company
Soggy Toast Company
MINT CHIP TECH
DISCRETIONARY TOY WORKSHOP

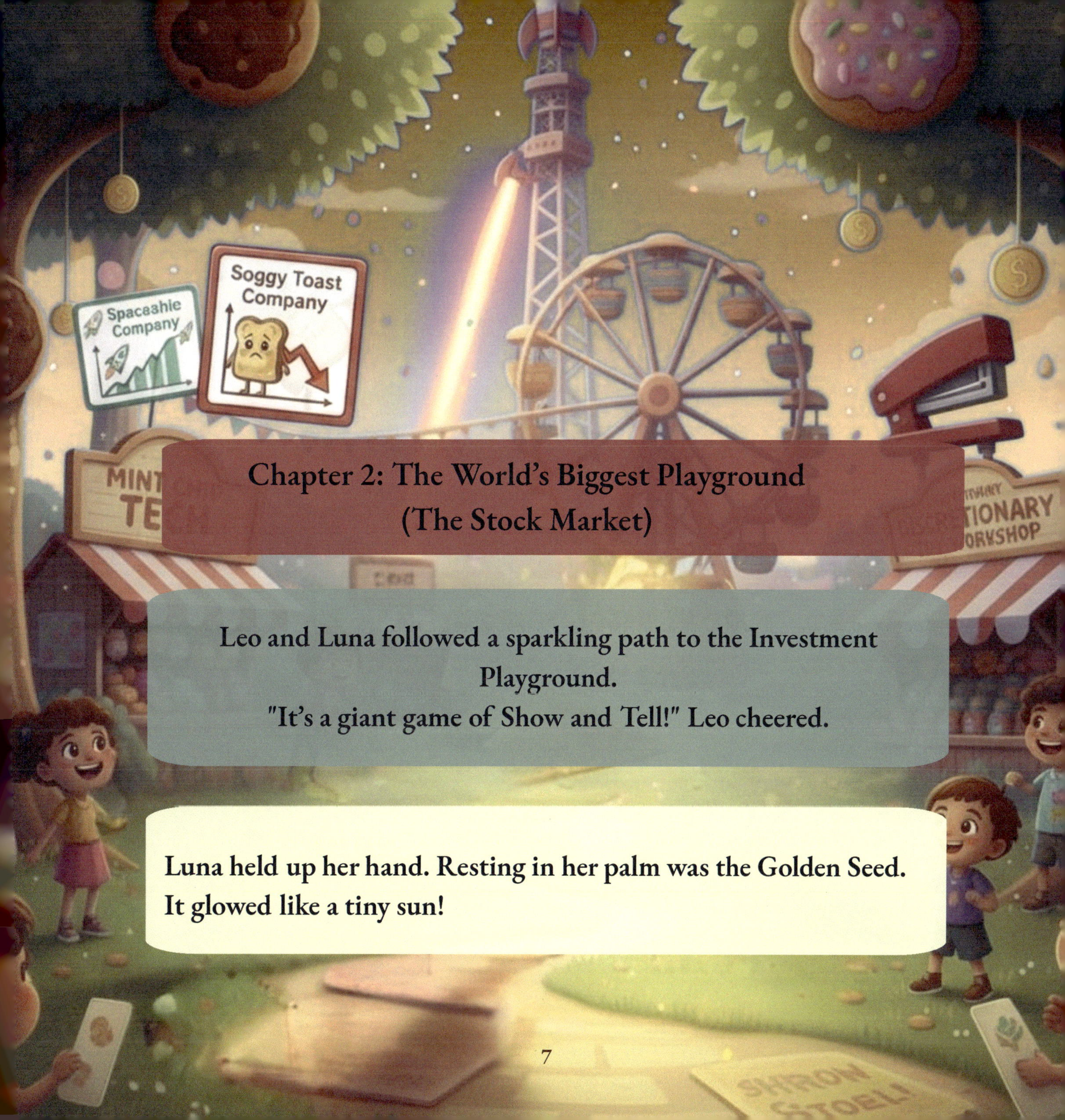

Chapter 2: The World's Biggest Playground (The Stock Market)

Leo and Luna followed a sparkling path to the Investment Playground.
"It's a giant game of Show and Tell!" Leo cheered.

Luna held up her hand. Resting in her palm was the Golden Seed. It glowed like a tiny sun!

If everybody wants a Spaceship,"
Luna said, "the price zooms up like
a rocket! "

But then she looked at Soggy Toast. He was very grumpy and very mushy.
"If nobody wants Soggy Toast," Luna sighed, "the price flops down like a wet noodle."

"Hmph!" grumped Soggy Toast. "I'm just waiting to get crisp!"

YOUR TURN: If you had to choose right now, would you trade your bean for a Robot Factory or a Cloud-Candy Shop? Point to your choice!

APL
D'S
DIS

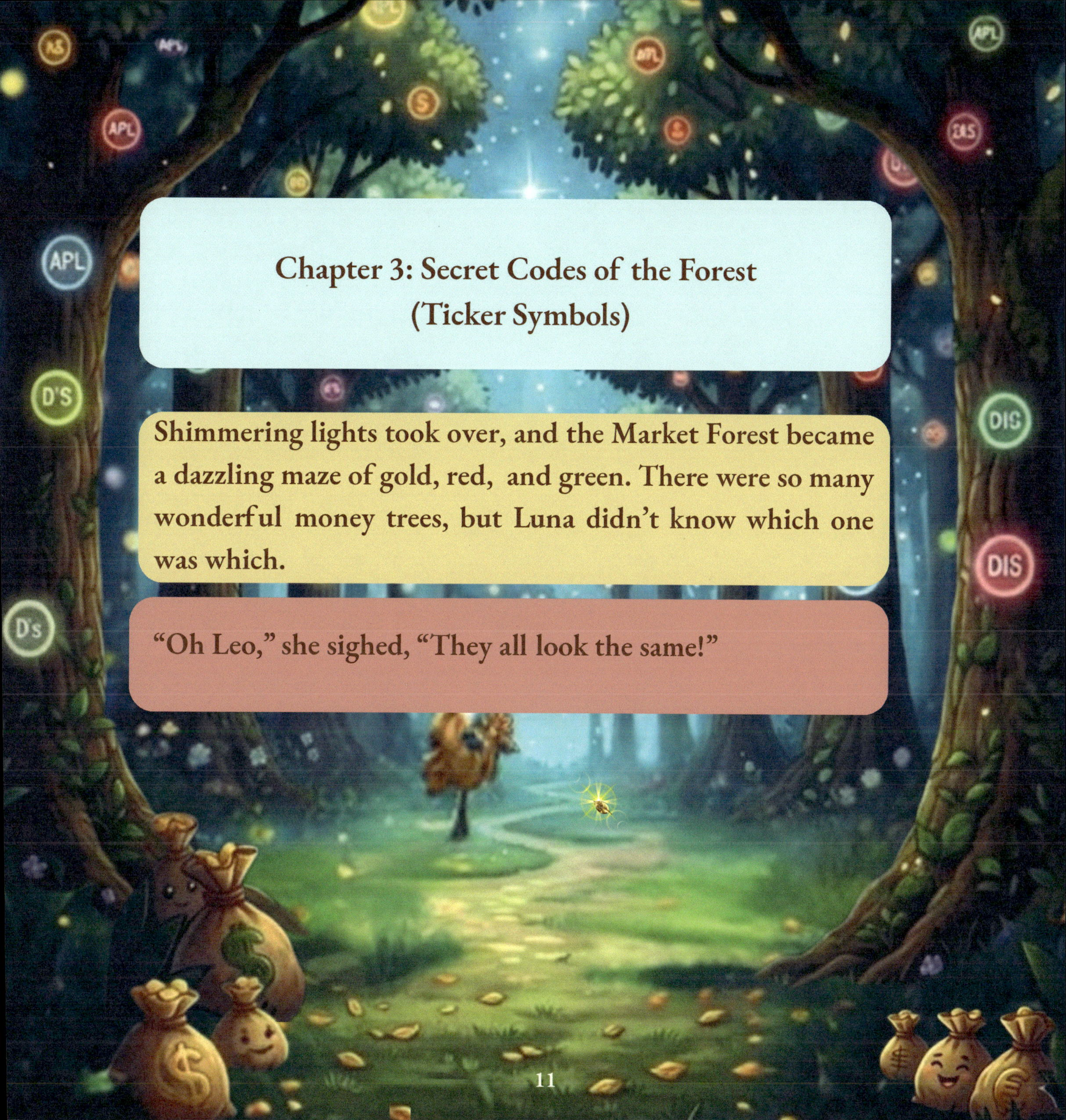

Chapter 3: Secret Codes of the Forest (Ticker Symbols)

Shimmering lights took over, and the Market Forest became a dazzling maze of gold, red, and green. There were so many wonderful money trees, but Luna didn't know which one was which.

"Oh Leo," she sighed, "They all look the same!"

APL
$
CRC

Leo smiled, pointing to a tiny, shimmering glow at the foot of a giant oak. “Not all of them, Luna. Look! That is a Magic Golden Bean. It is the rarest seed in the forest!

AAPL
DIS

To find more like it, Smart Gardeners use Secret Codes to keep their beans organized. These are called Ticker Symbols.

If you want to find the Apple tree,
you look for AAPL.

If you want the Disney tree, you look for DIS. These codes are like magical addresses—they help you find your beans in the giant Market Forest so you never get lost!”

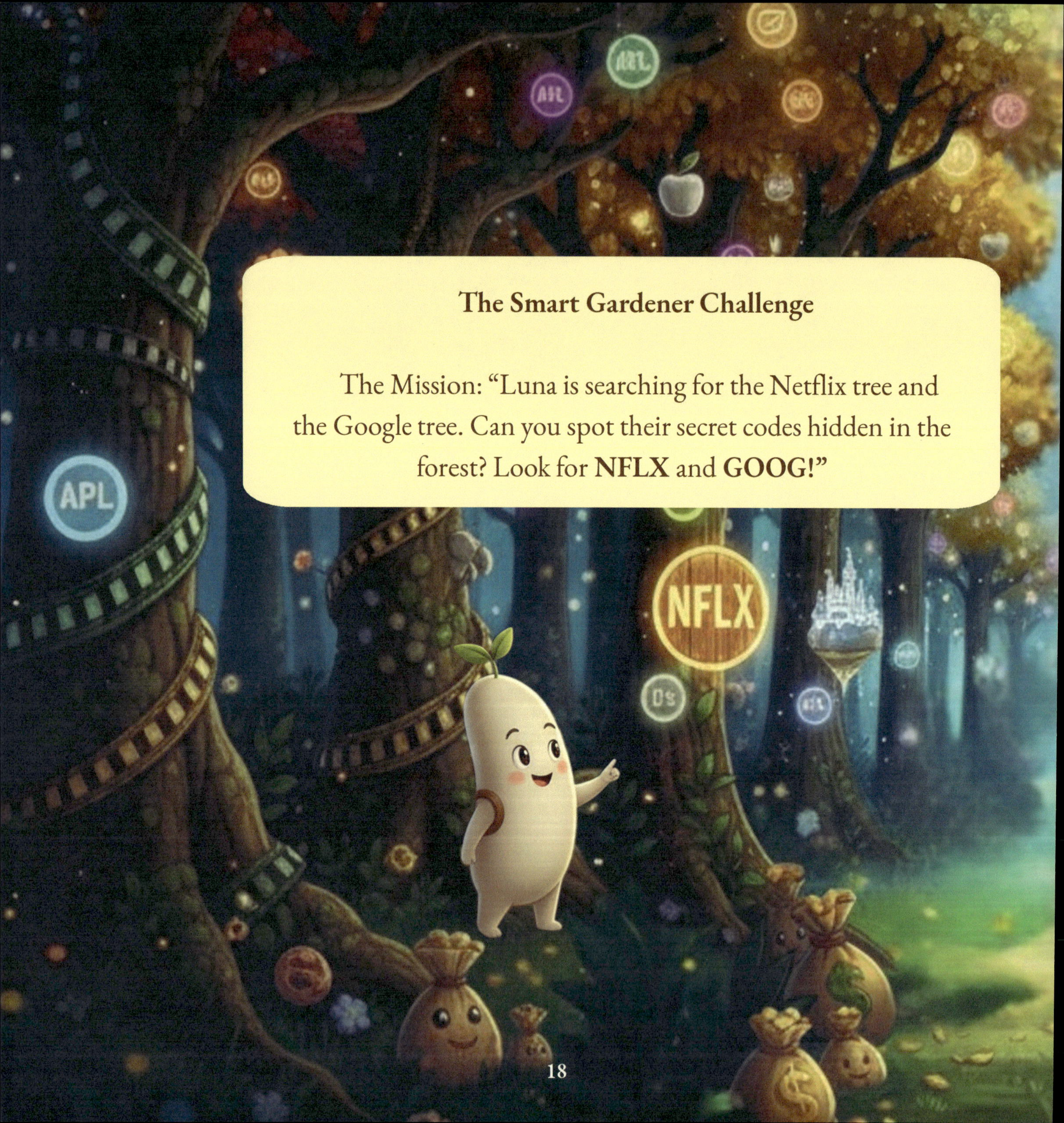

The Smart Gardener Challenge

The Mission: “Luna is searching for the Netflix tree and the Google tree. Can you spot their secret codes hidden in the forest? Look for **NFLX** and **GOOG!**”

Your Turn: "If you started a company that made Magic Space Boots, what would your 4-letter Secret Code be? Whisper your code to a friend, or keep it a secret just for your Smart Gardener notebook!

The Magic Cookie Factory

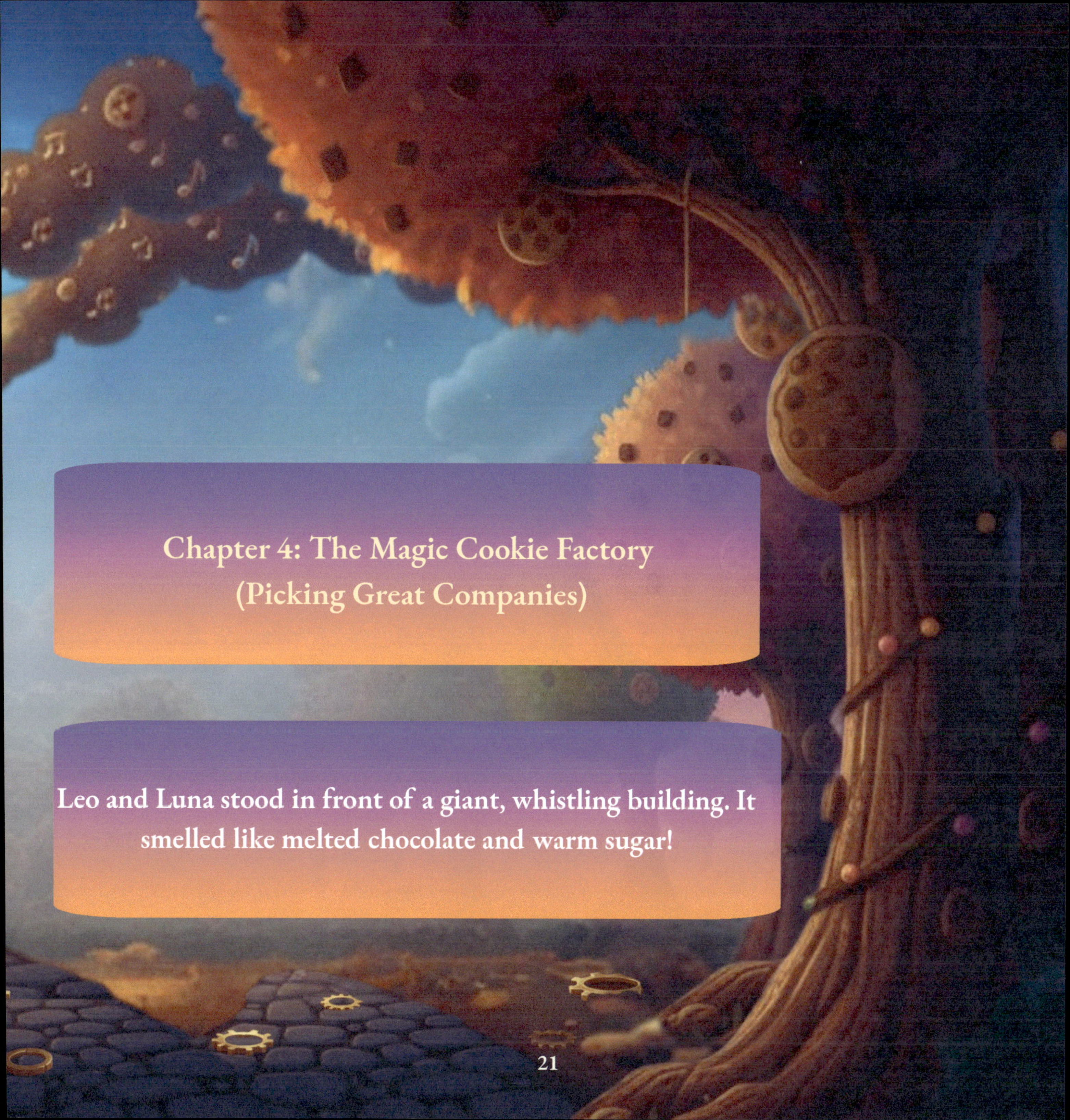

Chapter 4: The Magic Cookie Factory
(Picking Great Companies)

Leo and Luna stood in front of a giant, whistling building. It smelled like melted chocolate and warm sugar!

"This is a Company," Leo explained. "It's like a giant factory that makes things people love—like toys, games, or crunchy snacks!"

Luna held up her glowing seed.
"If the bakers do a great job and sell lots of cookies, our tiny 'seeds' grow bigger and stronger!"

But what if the cookies are burnt?" Leo asked.

"Then the seed stays small," Luna said

"A Smart Gardener looks for the factories with the best recipes!"

YOUR TURN: Imagine you are the boss of a Magic Factory! What is the one thing your factory would make to make people happy? Give your factory a name and shout it out loud!

GARDEN MAP

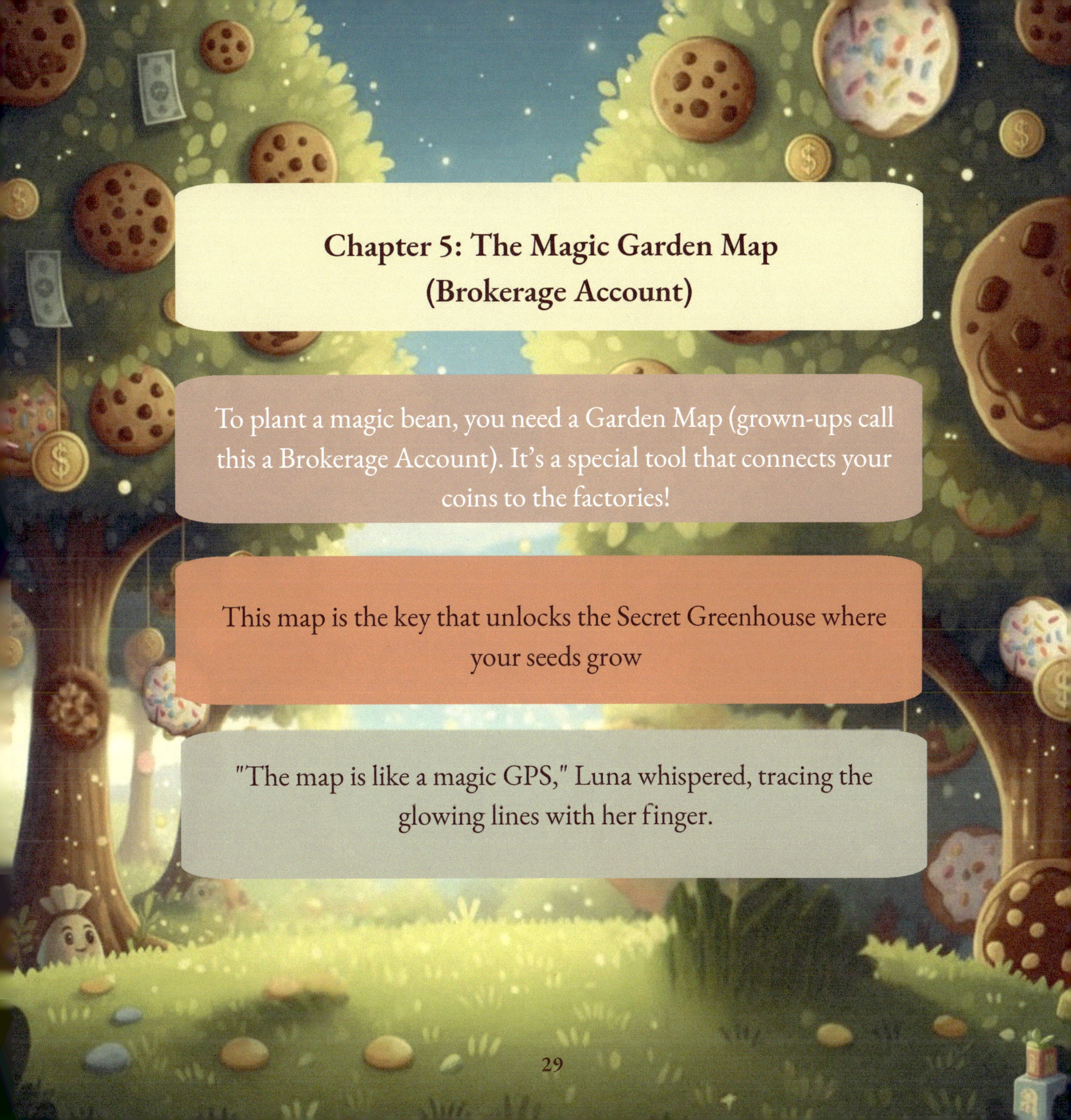

Chapter 5: The Magic Garden Map (Brokerage Account)

To plant a magic bean, you need a Garden Map (grown-ups call this a Brokerage Account). It's a special tool that connects your coins to the factories!

This map is the key that unlocks the Secret Greenhouse where your seeds grow

"The map is like a magic GPS," Luna whispered, tracing the glowing lines with her finger.

You tell the map exactly which factory you want to own, and it puts your name on a Magic Square.

Leo nodded, "That square is your proof! It tells the whole world that you are a real part-owner of that factory's land." Without your map, you wouldn't know where to dig!

YOUR TURN: Imagine you have a giant, invisible map floating in the air in front of you. Reach out and "tap" three different spots in the air to pick where your seeds will go. Boop! Boop! Boop! Now you've set your coordinates!

Chapter 6: The Garden Fence (Portfolio)

Leo and Luna stood back to look at their land. It wasn't just one bean anymore—it was a whole row of sprouting treasures!

"As you collect more seeds, you put them all together in your Portfolio," Leo said, stretching his arms wide. "Think of your Portfolio as your very own garden fence. Inside this fence is every single magic tree you own!"

Luna skipped along the fence line. "Some might be tall, some might be short, but together they make your forest strong! A Smart Gardener always keeps an eye on their Portfolio to see how the whole forest is growing together."

YOUR TURN: A Portfolio is a team of businesses! Stand up and pretend to build a fence around your room with your arms. Everything inside that fence is part of your powerful forest. How many "trees" (seeds) do you have in your forest so far? Count them out loud!

Chapter 7: The Secret of the Sun (Patience)

"Leo and Luna stood on the grass, watching their tiny sprouts. Suddenly, the air began to sparkle with gold dust. A beautiful lady appeared, walking so lightly that her feet didn't even touch the blades of grass. It was the Fairy Queen!

'The most important tool for a Master Gardener isn't a shovel,' Leo said, pointing to the Fairy's glowing wand. 'It's a clock!'Luna looked surprised. 'A clock?'

"Yes!" the Fairy whispered. "Magic trees don't grow in just one hour. They grow while you're at school, while you play, and even while you sleep. The longer you leave them in the sun, the bigger the treasure becomes!"

YOUR TURN: Growing a forest takes a lot of patience. Close your eyes and take one deep, slow breath. That is one second of "watering" your garden. If you can wait and be patient, how tall do you think your tree will grow? Reach your hands as high as you can!

The Moat

Chapter 8: The Magic Castle Moat
(Safety)

Leo pointed to a grand castle in the distance, surrounded by a deep, sparkling river.
"See that water, Luna? That's not just for swimming. That's a Moat!"

Luna tilted her head. "A Moat? Does it have dragons?"

The
Moat

"Maybe!" Leo laughed. "But it has something even bigger. Look at those giant splashes! That is The Whale. He is so big that when he swims, he moves the whole river!

His giant waves keep the castle safe and make sure only the best gardeners can reach the gates."

magic money beans

The Moat is a wall of safety," Leo explained. "It protects the factory's secrets, like a special cookie recipe. The Whale and the water make sure your magic beans stay tucked away where no one can grab them!"

YOUR TURN: Imagine you have a secret cookie recipe that tastes like starlight and rainbows. If you didn't want anyone else to find it, where would you hide it? Draw a tiny "Secret Key" in the corner of this page to lock your vault!

EYE SPY: Can you find the golden shield hidden in the castle wall? That shield represents a "Strong Brand"—it's a name people trust!

Chapter 9: Dancing in the Rain (Staying Calm)

Suddenly, the bright sky turned gray. CRACK-BOOM! Thunder rolled over the garden, and heavy rain began to fall.

Luna grabbed her sun hat. "Oh no, Leo! The garden is getting soaked! Will our money trees be okay?"

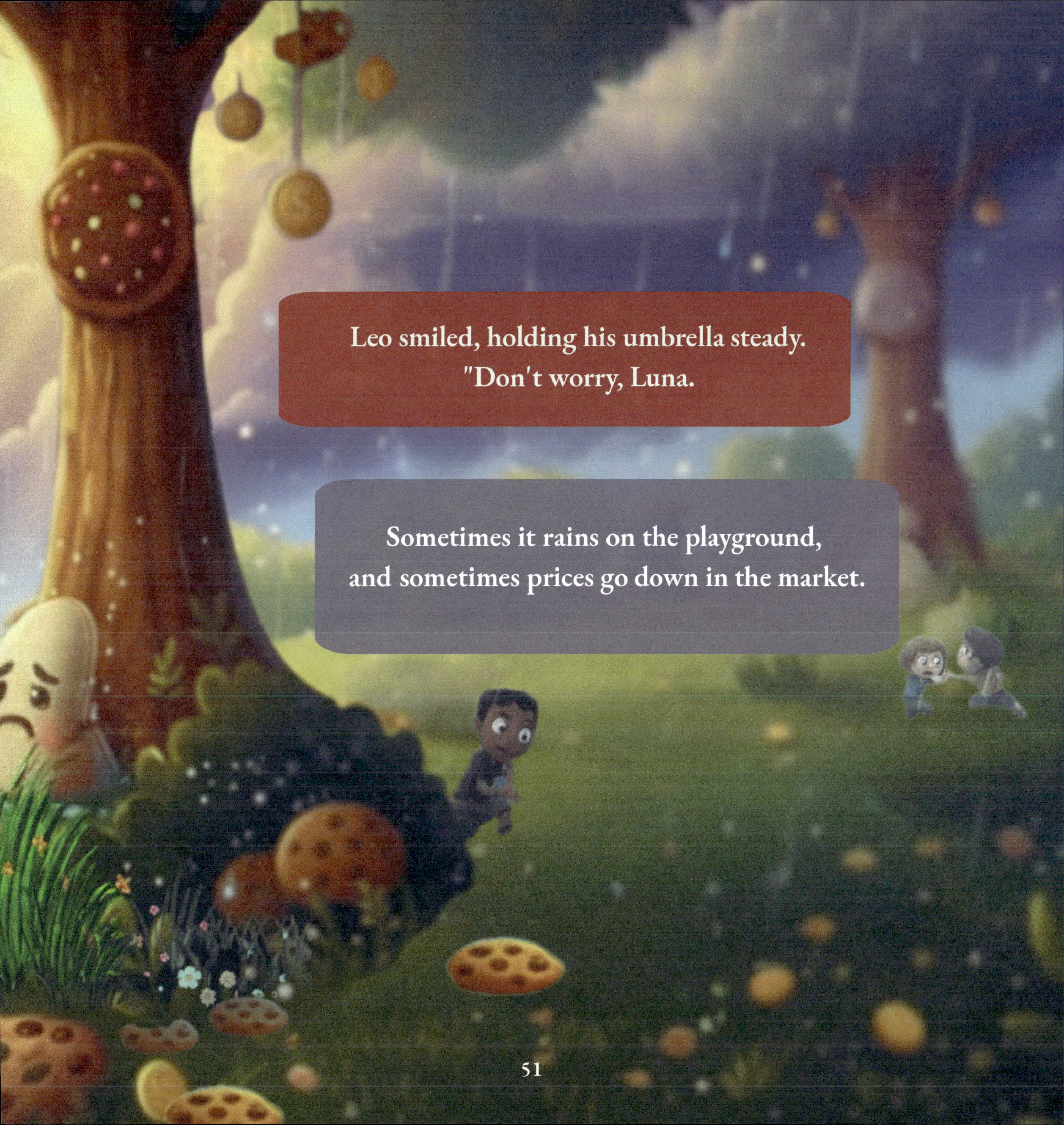

Leo smiled, holding his umbrella steady.
"Don't worry, Luna.

Sometimes it rains on the playground,
and sometimes prices go down in the market.

People get scared and want to run away,
but Smart Gardeners know a secret: Trees need rain to grow!"

Leo grabbed Luna's hand and did a little splashy twirl. "Instead of hiding, let's show the garden we aren't afraid.

Let's dance!" Luna giggled, following his lead. They splashed through the puddles, turning the scary storm into a rainy party.

We stay calm, hold onto our beans, and wait for the sun. The storm always passes, and the garden comes out even greener."

DEEP BREATH: When the "market storm" comes, the best thing to do is stay calm. Let's practice! Take a big breath in like you're smelling a flower... and blow it out like you're blowing away a rain cloud.

EYE SPY: Luna and Leo are hiding under a giant leaf! Can you find it? What else can you find that is staying dry in the rain?

Chapter 10: The Magic Cookie Party (Earning Dividends)

Some trees in the Market Forest are extra special.
When they grow big and strong and make lots of extra beans, they like to share!
This surprise gift is called a Dividend.

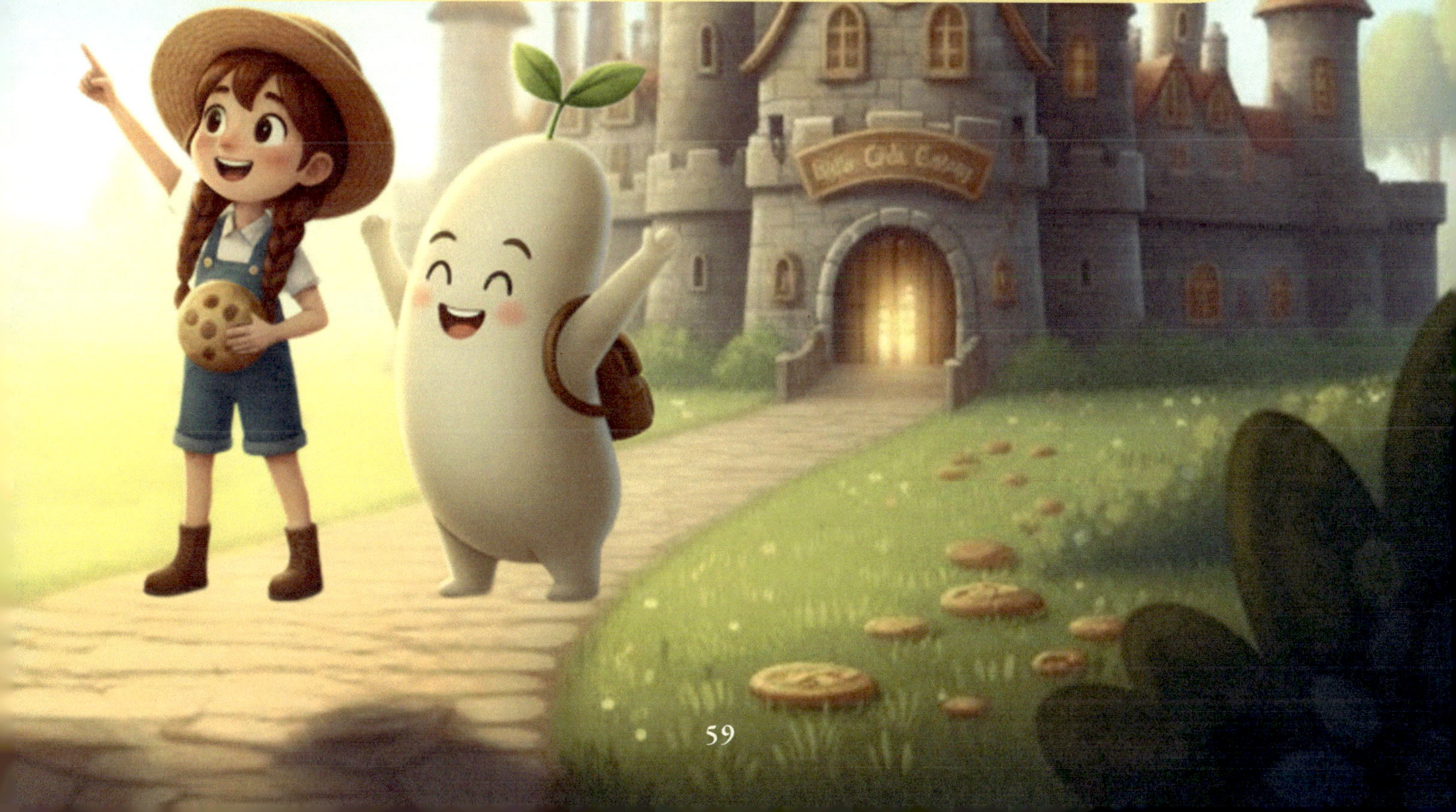

Dividend

Suddenly, a tiny bell rang!
Out marched the Money Bags team, wearing gold bowties and carrying silver trays.

"A Dividend is like a delicious 'Thank You' cookie delivered right to your porch by the Money Bags," Leo explained. "Just because you helped take care of the tree! The more pieces of the tree you own, the more cookies arrive at your door. It's a never-ending cookie party!"

The Smart Gardener Challenge

The Mission: "Luna's favorite tree just sent her 3 Dividend Cookies. If she gets 3 more tomorrow, how many cookies will she have for her party?"

Your Turn: "If a giant Chocolate Chip Factory sent you a 'Thank You' gift today, would you choose a box of cookies or a magic glass of milk? Tell your reading partner your choice!"

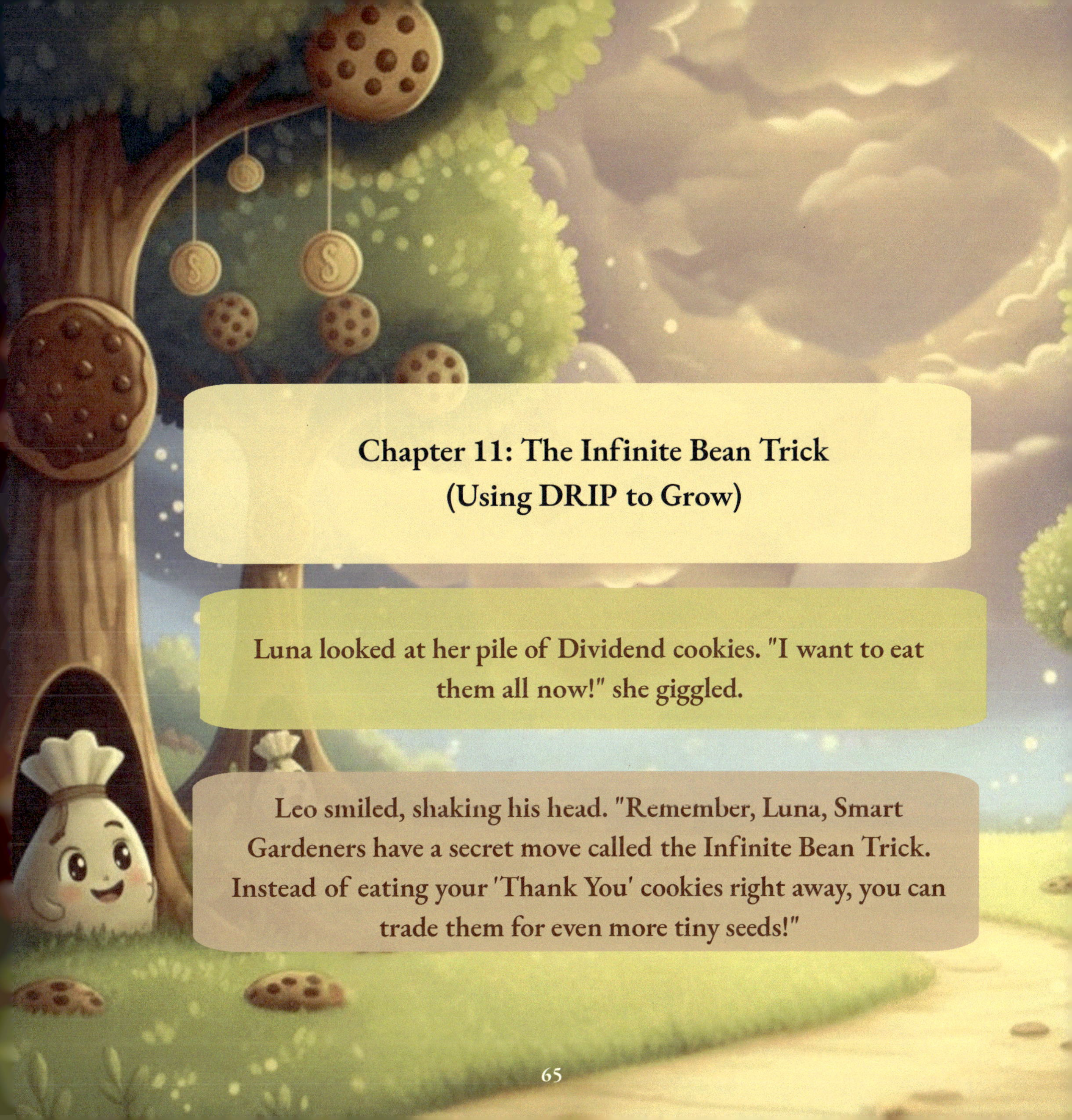

Chapter 11: The Infinite Bean Trick (Using DRIP to Grow)

Luna looked at her pile of Dividend cookies. "I want to eat them all now!" she giggled.

Leo smiled, shaking his head. "Remember, Luna, Smart Gardeners have a secret move called the Infinite Bean Trick. Instead of eating your 'Thank You' cookies right away, you can trade them for even more tiny seeds!"

Thank You
Thank You

Luna traded her cookies, and instantly, a group of tiny, glowing Happy Bean Sprouts popped out of the ground, cheering!

Leo showed her how to plant them back into her Portfolio. Now, Luna had more trees, which would make even more cookies.

This magical cycle is called DRIP. It's like a cookie that grows its own bakery!

The Smart Gardener Challenge

The Mission: "Luna has one cookie. If she uses the Infinite Bean Trick to get a new seed, and that seed grows into a tree that makes two cookies, how many cookies will she have next time?

Your Turn: "If you had a magic bag that doubled whatever you put inside, would you put a cookie, a toy car, or a shiny coin in first? Whisper your answer to Leo!"

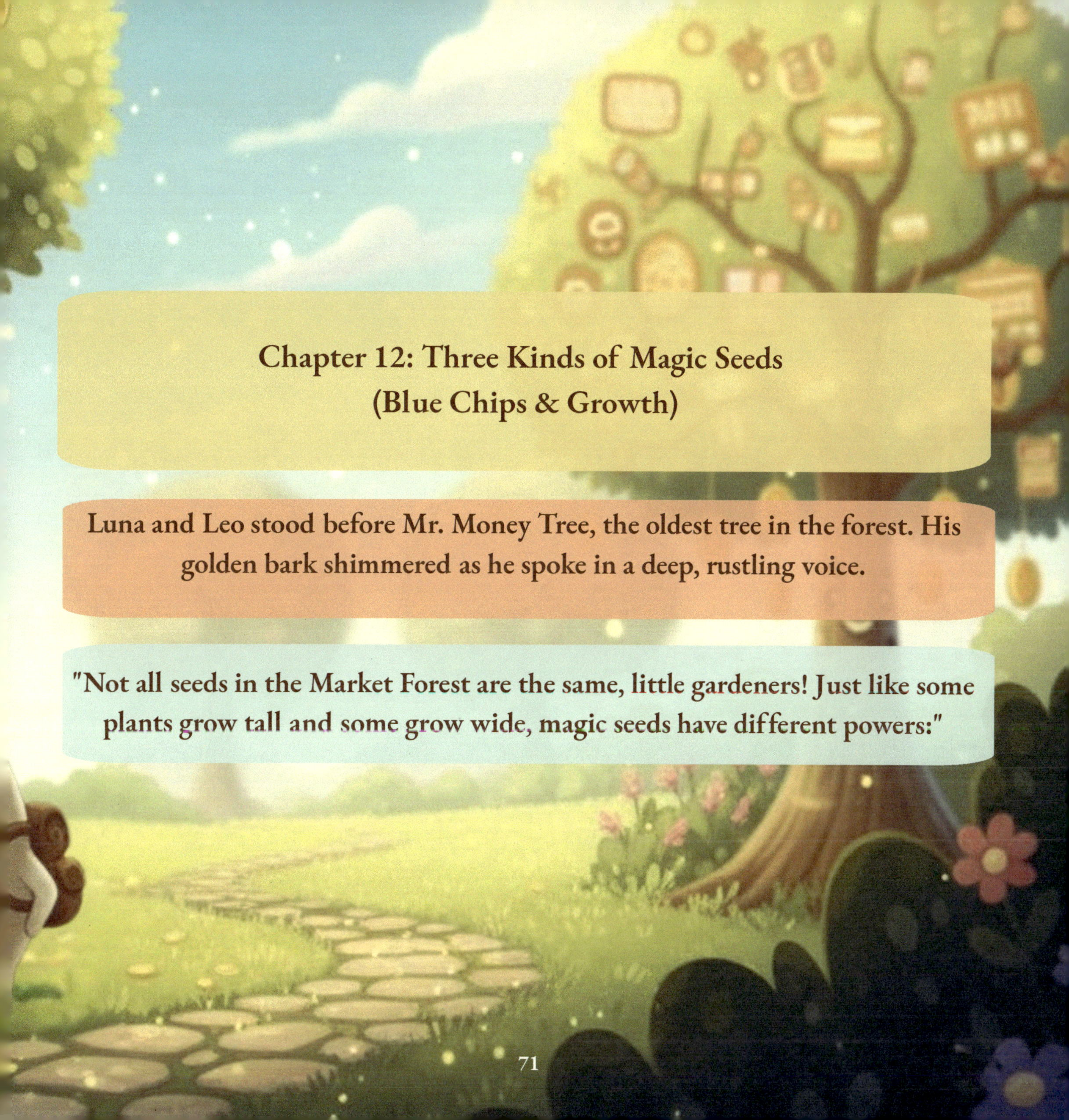

Chapter 12: Three Kinds of Magic Seeds (Blue Chips & Growth)

Luna and Leo stood before Mr. Money Tree, the oldest tree in the forest. His golden bark shimmered as he spoke in a deep, rustling voice.

"Not all seeds in the Market Forest are the same, little gardeners! Just like some plants grow tall and some grow wide, magic seeds have different powers:"

GameStop
(GAME)
KO
KO
KO
KO

Blue Chips: These are old, sturdy trees like Coca-Cola (KO). Mr. Money Tree loves them because they are famous for being super strong and giving out lots of "Thank You" cookies to everyone who helps them grow.

Growth Beans: These are like ONDS. They make flying robots! These trees grow very fast, but they usually keep their cookies so they can build even more robots.

Social Beans: These are like GameStop (GME). These seeds get famous because friends on the internet decide to have a big party and celebrate them all at once!

KO

The Smart Gardener Challenge

The Mission: “Luna wants to build a robot army. Which magic seed should she plant: a Blue Chip or a Growth Bean?”

Your Turn: “If you could plant a tree that grew anything, would you want it to grow strong and steady like a Blue Chip, or super fast like a Growth Bean? Tell Leo your plan!”

GME
KP
KO

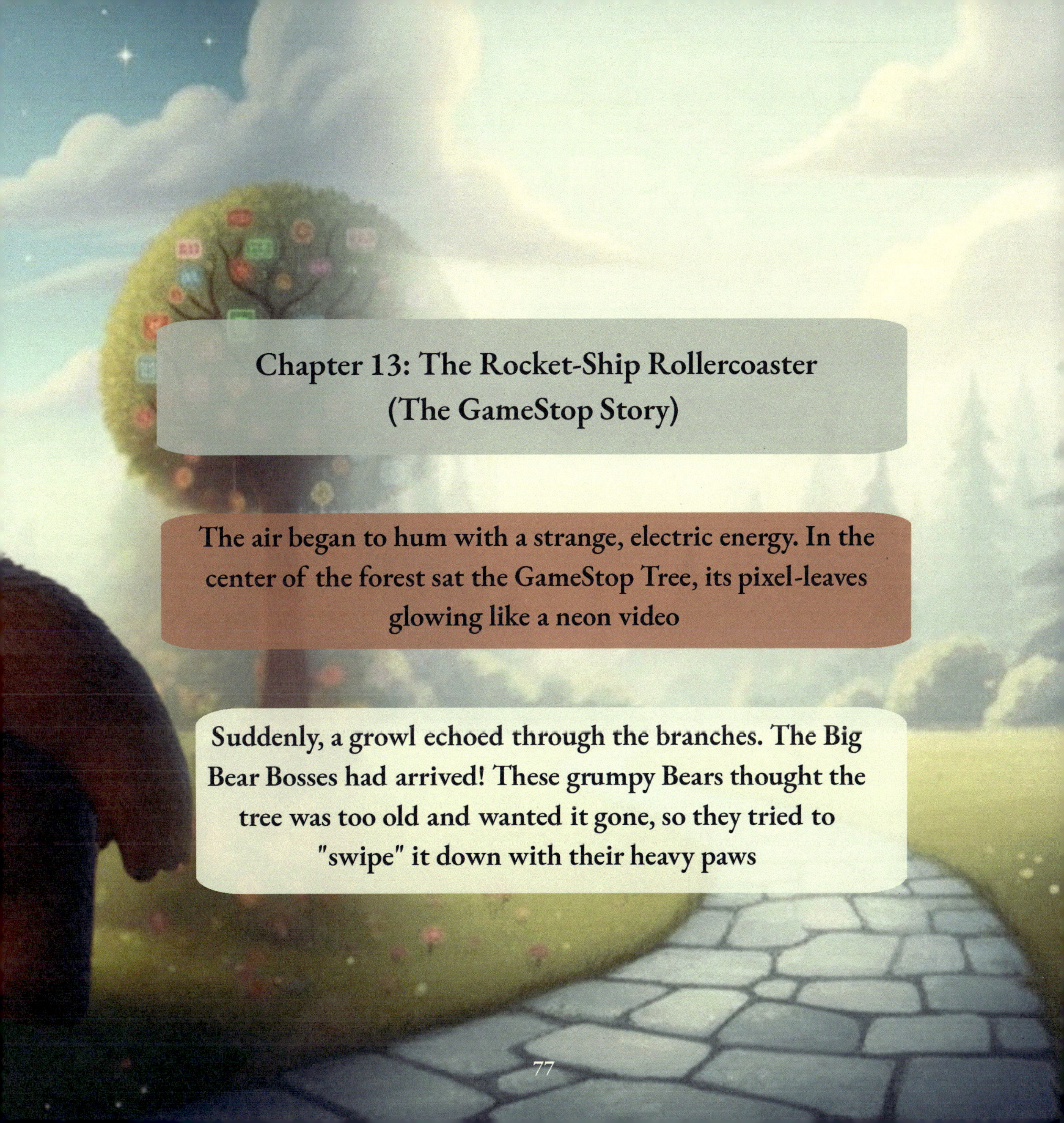

Chapter 13: The Rocket-Ship Rollercoaster (The GameStop Story)

The air began to hum with a strange, electric energy. In the center of the forest sat the GameStop Tree, its pixel-leaves glowing like a neon video

Suddenly, a growl echoed through the branches. The Big Bear Bosses had arrived! These grumpy Bears thought the tree was too old and wanted it gone, so they tried to "swipe" it down with their heavy paws

GME
KO
APPL
GME
GME
KO

But then, a giant group of friends—just like you!—
shouted, "NO!" They hugged the tree so hard that it
turned into a Rocket Ship and blasted past the Bears!

Luna and Leo noticed that the higher the rocket went, the faster it shook. It was a "Social Bean," which meant it could zoom to the stars one minute and drop like a stone the next when the Bears started swiping again!

GME
9
STRONG
SEEDS

The Smart Gardener's Secret

"Whoa," Leo said, catching his breath. "That rocket move was exciting, but a little scary!" Luna nodded. "That's the risk, Leo. Social Beans are like playing on a trampoline—it's fun, but if you're not careful, you can fall off."

The Golden Rule: Never plant more "Social Beans" than you can afford to lose. If you have ten seeds, keep nine of them for your strong, steady trees. Only use one seed for the rollercoaster ride. That way, even if the rocket comes back down, your forest is still safe!

Chapter 14: The Flavor Sectors (Learning Sectors)

After the wild ride of the GameStop Rollercoaster, Luna and Leo took a deep breath. Their hearts were still racing!

"Phew," Luna said, wiping her forehead. "I like the excitement, but I think my tummy needs something a little more steady."

Mr. Money Tree smiled. "A healthy forest needs many flavors to stay strong!

We grow our trees in neighborhoods called Sectors. That way, if one flavor has a 'melty' day, the others stay cool and delicious. Ready to see the four flavors that keep our garden growing?

Tech (Mint Chip): The Inventors!

These trees grow the coolest gadgets and flying robots.
They are the fastest-growing trees in the whole Market Forest!

SOFT SNIFFLES
YUMMY OATS

Staples (Vanilla):

The Needs! Everyone needs these daily, like soap and snacks.

These are the "Everyday Trees." They grow the things we use every single morning and every single night—like bubbly soap, minty toothpaste, and yummy snacks. Because everyone needs these every day, the Vanilla neighborhood is a very busy and happy place!

Wants (Bubblegum): The Fun Stuff! These trees grow toys, games, and treats.

Pop! Zip! Zoom! The Bubblegum trees are bursting with toys! While the Vanilla trees give us what we need, the Bubblegum trees grow what we love. It's a magical world of pink leaves and play-pretend, where every branch holds a brand-new toy for a lucky gardener!

Health (Strawberry): The Helpers! These trees grow medicine to keep the forest healthy.

From sticky band-aids to vitamin treats, these trees are full of "Healthy Magic." They are the strong red anchors of the forest that make sure everyone stays happy, healthy, and full of energy!

MINT CHIP
BUBBGLEGUM
STRAWBERRY
NEEDS
Wants
NEEDS
Tech

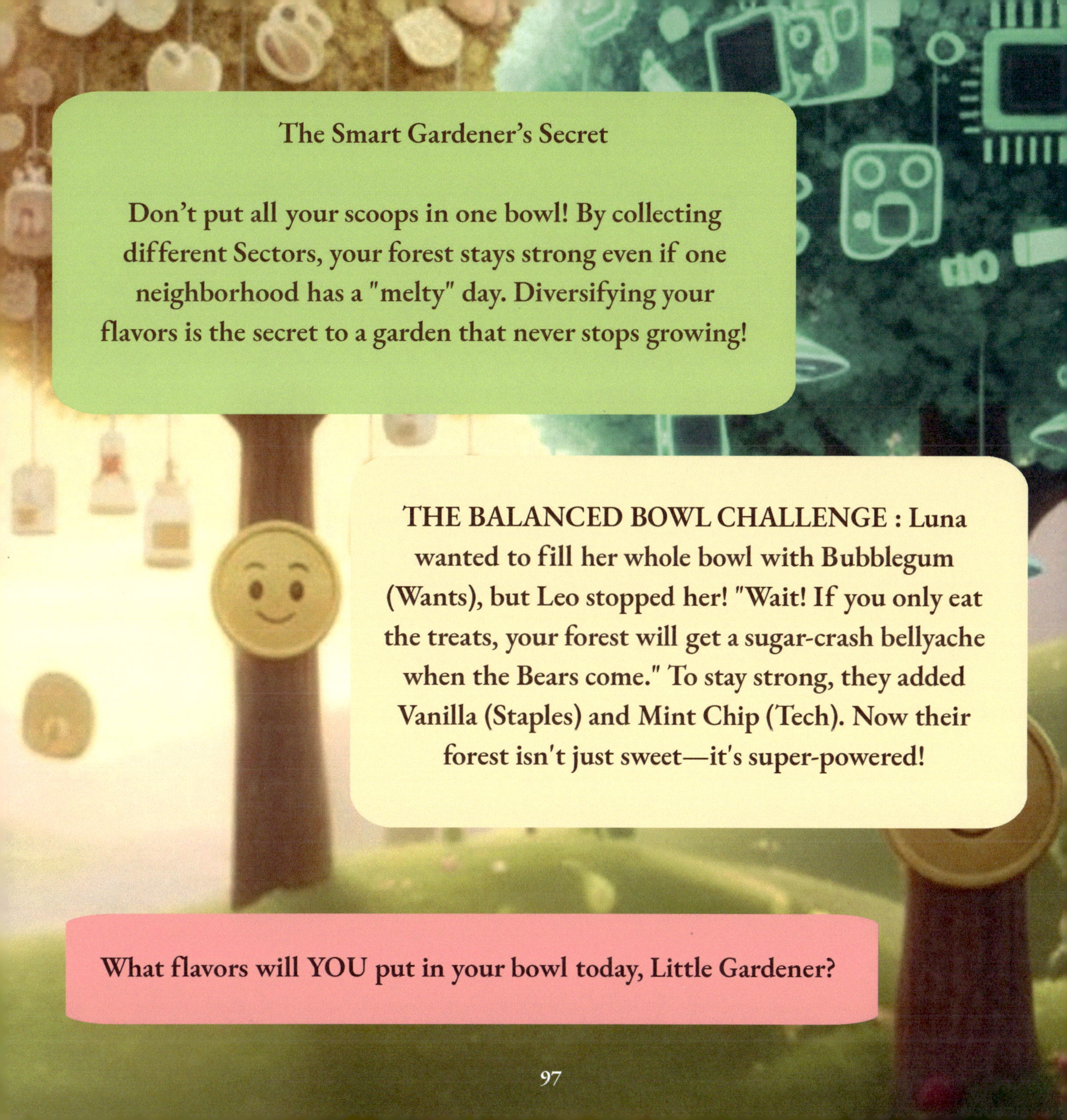

The Smart Gardener's Secret

Don't put all your scoops in one bowl! By collecting different Sectors, your forest stays strong even if one neighborhood has a "melty" day. Diversifying your flavors is the secret to a garden that never stops growing!

THE BALANCED BOWL CHALLENGE : Luna wanted to fill her whole bowl with Bubblegum (Wants), but Leo stopped her! "Wait! If you only eat the treats, your forest will get a sugar-crash bellyache when the Bears come." To stay strong, they added Vanilla (Staples) and Mint Chip (Tech). Now their forest isn't just sweet—it's super-powered!

What flavors will YOU put in your bowl today, Little Gardener?

Chapter 15: The Variety Treat Basket (What is an ETF?)

Leo and Luna are exploring the Candy Forest, but the trees are acting wild! Some grow Sweet chocolate, while others grow Bitter licorice, Tart lemons, or even Sour limes.

"How do we pick the sweets without getting a mouth full of sour?" Luna asks. "Don't choose just one tree," says Leo. "Grab a Magic Basket!"

In the Market Forest, this basket is an ETF. Instead of picking one bean at a time, this basket lets you own a tiny piece of the whole Garden at once!

The Master Gardener's Secret

The Basket is your Shield! If you grab only one Bitter licorice, your snack is ruined. But in a Magic Basket, the Sweet cookies balance out the Sour lemons. An ETF makes sure your Garden stays delicious, even if a few trees turn tart!

Your Turn!

If your Magic Basket could hold four flavors, what would they be?

Something Sweet:

Something Tart: ____________

Something Sour: ____________

Something Bitter: ___________

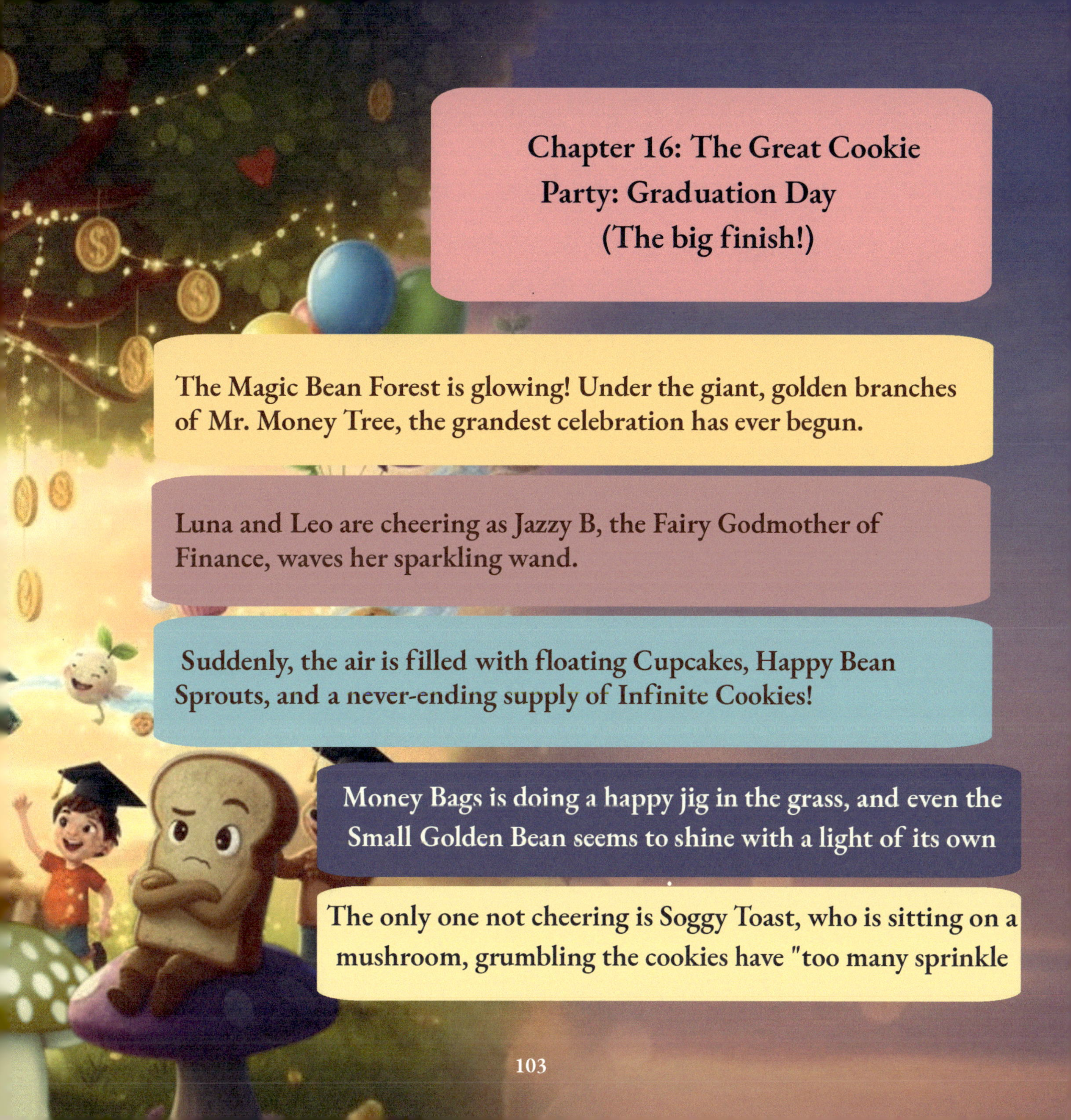

Chapter 16: The Great Cookie Party: Graduation Day (The big finish!)

The Magic Bean Forest is glowing! Under the giant, golden branches of Mr. Money Tree, the grandest celebration has ever begun.

Luna and Leo are cheering as Jazzy B, the Fairy Godmother of Finance, waves her sparkling wand.

Suddenly, the air is filled with floating Cupcakes, Happy Bean Sprouts, and a never-ending supply of Infinite Cookies!

Money Bags is doing a happy jig in the grass, and even the Small Golden Bean seems to shine with a light of its own

The only one not cheering is Soggy Toast, who is sitting on a mushroom, grumbling the cookies have "too many sprinkle

The Forest Guardians, The Bull & The Bear, are there too! The Bull uses his strong horns to push the cookie prices up high,

while the Bear uses his heavy paws to swipe them down low.
But don't worry—your forest is strong enough for both!

Luna whispers, "We didn't just plant seeds, Leo." Leo holds his bean high toward the clouds: "We built a whole Forest!"

You've done it, Smart Gardener! Look how your forest has grown:

The Entrance: You found your bean and unlocked your Magic Map (Brokerage Account).

The Strategy: You built a Giant's Wall (The Moat) to keep your Castles safe.

The Magic Sun: You learned that Patience is the sun that grows the tallest trees.

The Growth: You mastered the Infinite Bean Trick (DRIP) for a never-ending feast!

The Wisdom: You learned to Dance in the Rain and used a Magic Basket (ETF) to stay balanced.

The Future: You now have the tools to turn one tiny bean into a legacy that reaches the stars!

Remember: The best gardens aren't grown overnight. Even the tallest money trees in the Market Forest started as a single seed.
Keep learning, keep planting, and watch your future bloom!

MEET THE RESIDENTS
(The Character Bible)

Jazzy B™: The Fairy Queen Head Gardener and Guide who shows you how to grow your own Golden Bean Forest.

Luna™: The Chief Liquidity Officer in her straw hat.She uses her aluminum watering jug to grow the forest!

Leo™: The Market Watcher. A white lima bean with a leather backpack. His Magic Sprout points to the best stocks.

The Magic Golden Bean™: A tiny, faceless bean that glows with pure gold. It is the rarest seed in the forest and represents the ultimate goal of a Smart Gardener!

Mr. Money Tree™: The ancient oak with a wise face. Catchphrase: "Roots in the research, fruits in the pocket."

Soggy Toast™: The always grumpy veteran. He reminds us to stay "crisp" so we don't get burned!

MEET THE RESIDENTS
(The Character Bible)

The Bull™: The Forest Guardian, The Bull uses his strong horns to toss cookie prices toward the moon!

The Bear™: He uses his heavy paws to swipe prices down so we can plant more seeds!

The Whale™: The giant of the deep blue market. He is so big that when he swims, he creates waves that move all the other little fish!

Money Bags™: The Forest's Champion Organizer. Keeping Golden Beans safe and handing out "Tree-Treats" (Dividends).

Happy Bean Sprouts™ The Forest's Ultimate Cheer Squad! Celebrating every new leaf and dancing whenever your wealth grows.

The Magic Bean Academy
MAGIC BEAN ACADEMY

THE COOKIE GLOSSARY

Brokerage Account: Your "Garden Map" that connects your coins to the factories and shows you where your Magic Squares are planted.

Dividend: A "Thank You" cookie sent to you by a company for being a partner and owning a share.

DRIP: The Infinite Bean Trick—automatically turning your earned cookies back into new seeds to grow more trees.

ETF: A Magic Basket that holds a group of many different stocks so you can own them all at once.

Moat: A Giant Wall or Water Moat built around a Castle (Company) to keep it safe from competitors.

Portfolio: Your collection of magic trees and plants kept safely together inside your garden fence.

Sector Diversification: Planting a mix of different factories (like Cookies and Toys) so your garden stays strong even if one factory slows down.

Ticker: A company's secret nickname (like AAPL for Apple) used to find them on your Garden Map.

Jazzy B's Dividend Delights
Featuring Luna & Leo's Magic Seeds

Prep time: 10 mins | Bake time: 10 mins | Yields: 24 "Magic Cookies"

In the Magic Bean Academy, we celebrate our growing trees with a treat! Grab a Grown-Up Portfolio Manager (an adult) and let's bake!"

The Ingredients:

- **1 cup softened butter (The "Sunshine")**
- **1 cup brown sugar (The "Soil")**
- **1 egg (The "Life Force")**
- **2 cups flour (The "Magic Dust")**
- **1 tsp baking soda**
- **The Seeds: 1 cup of mixed chocolate, butterscotch, and white chips!**
- **1 pinch Coarse Sea Salt (The "Diversification Balance")**

The Instructions:

1. **Preheat your oven to 350°F.**
2. **Mix the sunshine, soil, and egg in a big bowl until creamy.**
3. **Stir in the magic dust and baking soda.**
4. **Fold in your "seeds" (the chips).**
5. **Scoop small balls onto a tray and bake for 10 minutes until golden.**

The Magic Secret: Sprinkle the **Diversification Balance** on top while warm to protect your profits!

Did You Know? A **Dividend** is like a cookie that a company gives you just for owning a "Magic Bean" (a share)! Share these with another Smart Gardener to grow your friendship portfolio.

Meet the Author: Jazzy B

Jazzy B is the Chief Gardener at the Magic Bean Academy. With a passion for planting big ideas in small pockets, Jazzy B believes that every child has the potential to grow their own money into a magical forest of opportunity.

When not exploring the Investment Playground or scouting for the next great Cookie Factory, Jazzy B can be found teaching future Smart Gardeners that patience, curiosity, and a little bit of magic are the most important tools in any portfolio.

This is Jazzy B's first guide in the Academy series, dedicated to making the world of finance as fun as a day at the park and ensuring that the next generation of Smart Gardeners grows up with the confidence to turn their tiny seeds into a blooming future.

"To all the little gardeners out there: Your dreams are the seeds. Your patience is the water.

Never stop growing!" — Jazzy B

The Parent's Master Gardener Guide

How to Open a Custodial Account in 3 Easy Steps

Step 1: Choose Your "Soil" (The Broker) Pick a platform to hold your "Magic Beans." Popular options include **Fidelity Youth, Charles Schwab,** or **Robinhood.** Robinhood is very easy to use on your phone! Look for a **UTMA** or **UGMA account—these are special accounts owned by the child but managed by you.**

Step 2: Plant the Seed You will need the child's Social Security Number and your own ID. Most accounts can be opened online in under 10 minutes with as little as $1 to start.

Step 3: Invite the Whole Family! Grandparents, aunts, and uncles can all help the forest grow! Most custodial accounts allow family members to make **direct deposits or "** gift" shares of stock for birthdays and holidays. Instead of a toy that might break, they can give a "Magic Bean" that grows forever.

Pro-Tip for Parents: Set up an "Automatic Transfer" of $10 or $20 a month. Even small amounts grow into a massive forest over time thanks to the power of **Compound Interest!**

The Magic Bean Hall of Fame

The Tech Garden

Apple (AAPL): The creators of iPhones and big ideas.
Pays Dividends? Yes

Nintendo (NTDOY): The home of Mario and legendary video games.
Pays Dividends? Yes

Roblox (RBLX): A digital world where kids create and play.
Pays Dividends? Not yet

The Needs Garden

General Mills (GIS): Makers of Cheerios and Lucky Charms.
Pays Dividends? Yes

Coca-Cola (KO): The world's most famous treats and juices.
Pays Dividends? Yes

Hershey's (HSY): Making the world sweeter with chocolate bars.
Pays Dividends? Yes

The Wants Garden

Disney (DIS): The masters of movies and theme parks.
Pays Dividends? Yes

McDonald's (MCD): The most famous burger garden in the world.
Pays Dividends? Yes

Amazon (AMZN): The "Magic Package" delivery service.
Pays Dividends? Not yet

The Health Garden

Johnson & Johnson (JNJ): Makers of Band-Aids and medicine.
Pays Dividends? Yes

CVS Health (CVS)The Neighborhood Care Center The place families go for medicine, vitamins, and snacks. Pays Dividends? Yes

Walgreens (WBA)The Corner Drugstore Helping kids stay healthy with medicine and everyday essentials. Pays Dividends? Yes

MAGIC BEAN ACADEMY
GRADUATION DIPLOMA
Your Name Here!
You've grown so tall and learned so much,
with magic seeds and a money tree's touch!
This is for planting the best seeds,
and understanding 'The 10 Seeds Rule.'
You are now a certified, official: SMART GARDENER.
Luna
Luna, co-Founder
Leo
Leo, co-Founder
Signed: Jazzy B
DATE:
This is a happy novelty diploma for fun!

Made in the USA
Monee, IL
05 November 2026

67378003R00081